Title: Beautifully Imperfect

Subtitle: Beautifully Broken, Beautifully Human

Author: Steven Zilberg

Table of Contents

“You call it madness, but I call it love.”

(Unknown)

Short Story 1: Fireflies & 45 Years

It is a quarter after six. Sun has just begun to rest upon the horizon. Fiery oranges and reds. A mix of blues, greens, and purples paint the night sky. Stars have begun to shine. The moon beginning to wave from on-high. As your eyes begin to pan from the small acre of land to an even smaller plot; vegetables are growing, livestock are resting, and dogs are protecting cattle.

Fireflies dance 10 feet away from an elderly man's front door. His land. His property. His cattle. His dogs. All reflect his past, lessons learned, and his future.

He is peacefully resting on the porch. Walking stick crafted from a tree that has blessed the land for hundreds of years. Engraved with every tear, every smile, every laugh, and every footstep taken from birth until death visits his front door. An empty glass of lemonade sits upon the porch rail. From inside the home, footsteps are heard. They are neither heavy nor light footed.

The man's eyes reflect that of a young man. His gray hair and wrinkles reflect differently. His hands shake uncontrollably. He begins to stand, taking slow step after slow step. 10 minutes later he is kneeling in front of his two dogs who are on watch duty due to coyotes. Instead of standing back up, he sits against an oak tree.

After a couple minutes an old lady walks from inside the house onto the porch.

"Honey."

She notices the empty glass of lemonade sitting on the porch rail. She mutters to herself; 'damn fool left his glass on the porch again.'

Instead of returning inside she grabs the old man's walking stick that he left next to his rocking chair. She knows her husband like the back of her hand. They have been married for 47 years. Both would agree; 'we wouldn't change a damn thing."

Some days were easy. Some days were difficult. Some days consisted one of them causing the other to cry. Some days consisted of one of them raising their voice at the other. Some days consisted of both not listening to what the other way saying.

Despite the mountains. Despite the terrain. Despite the storms.

Everyday consisted of unconditional love. Everyday consisted of forgiveness. Everyday consisted of warm embraces. Everyday consisted of apologies, striving to improve, and putting in effort to better one another.

As the elder lady walks up to her husband; you notice the husband's scar. One above one of his eyes. Another on his back. His beard is neat, trimmed, and he is smiling. He is barefoot. Dirty jeans, white t-shirt. Both dogs resting their heads on his lap. One of his horses are grazing behind him.

You notice his demeanor. Peaceful. Not worried about his safety. Not worried about what his neighbors think of him or his old lady. He isn't worried about what the world thinks of him. He isn't worried about what others post online, what they say, or what they believe.

His mind is elsewhere. His dogs are resting. His mind has built a sanctuary within a sanctuary. His old lady greets him.

"Hey old man. Need some company?"

He doesn't need to answer. They've become so accustomed to each other's body language that they can finish each other's sentences, complete each other's thoughts, and know what the other is thinking.

She sits next to him.

"What are you thinking?"

It takes a minute for him to articulate his thoughts. His mind is still sharp. He collects his thoughts at a slower pace compared to 30 years ago.

"Honey, do you remember the day we met? I don't mean the vague details. Do you remember the feeling you were feelings that day?"

His old lay not sure of how to answer his question. Not because she can't but because she wants to be able to understand why he is asking what he is asking…

The old man continues.

"I remember that day like it was this morning. You were walking down the hall. Meeting your new co-workers. I had been having a stressful day. My mind was elsewhere. As I opened the door of my office; I saw you walking my way…"

His hands begun to shake uncontrollably again. His two dogs noticed. His old lady as well. She laid her hands upon his.

"Continue honey. I am listening."

So, he continued.

"It might be cheesy, but I don't give a damn. Love doesn't need to make sense, nor does it have to be complicated. I knew within 60 seconds of us meeting; that you were the other half of my soul. I knew you were the other half of my heart."

His old lady playfully laughed and asked.

"How did you know?"

He answered.

"It isn't about 'knowing'. It never was. It never will be. It has always been about believing. It will always be about faith. I never visited outer space. I never witnessed the devil himself or God in the flesh. Yet, I still believe in all three. The same is true with love."

He asks his old lady.

"What do you think is the most beautiful aspect of love?"

She replies.

"I don't know baby. Tell me."

The old man smiles wide. He points to their horses. He points to sun dipping below the horizon. He points to their home. He caresses his old lady's cheek and kisses her neck.

"When we are in the moment. We often search for proof. The most beautiful aspect of love is that proof is found later in life as you look back on the past. We built this house together. We have been married for 45 years. We have fought. We have argued. We never gave up on each other.

In my eyes you look as beautiful now as the first day I met you. You still are that bright eyes, gentle soul, always finding the good in others, and hand extended to others type of lady.

Your hair is as beautiful now as it was when it was full of color. Your eyes are as beautiful now as they were when we both had less wrinkles. Your skin is as beautiful now as it was when we used to lay in bed and caress each other's chest.

Despite life. Despite negativity. Despite disagreements. Despite others trying to break us apart. We stuck together. We wiped away each other's tears. We counseled each other. We advised one another.

That my dear is the most beautiful aspect of love.

That my dear is how we prove that love exists."

After the old man finishes his thoughts. Their two dogs stand at attention. His old lady assists him to his feet. She allows him to hold onto one of her arms. She leads him gently back to the house. They both disappear as the porch door closes.

Poem 2: You Are Loved

While we walk, run, and struggle. We meet folks who might be good, might be helpful, sometimes they might be not-so-good. It isn't a question of whether we should have stayed away, attempted to run, or tried to ignore. Rather, the Great Spirit always has its reasons.

…

For example, I could have stayed spiteful. Kept hating and wishing pain upon those who lied, stole, and hurt me. In grade school and high school, I was bullied. In college, I was sexually assaulted in a mosque parking lot. I have been treated like I am 'crazy'. I have been stereotypes as being 'dangerous' because I talk to myself out loud. I have been heartbroken by both girlfriends, boyfriends, and ambiguous confused snowflakes., I have fallen, scraped my knee, and walked barefoot alone.

…

I remember days when my pops became drunk and disorderly. I remember days waking up confused; not knowing where I was, how I got to where I was, and why I was where I was…

I remember being broke, homeless, and eating at church food kitchens on a nightly basis.

…

It took me 30 years to learn the truth. We hurt ourselves the most; the longer we hold onto hate, spite, and anger. It doesn't matter who did what, whose fault it was, or how bad they hurt you. The longer you hold onto that pain. The longer you refuse to forgive both yourself as well as them. The longer the pain persists. The longer your anxiety will linger. The longer your depression will exist.

…

People don't walk into our lives for no reason. God reminds us we are always growing, learning, forgiving, and reflecting. The number of times I have been lied to, taken for a fool, and perceived to be weak.

...

One of the most beautiful aspects of life; our ability to choose, forgive, and move-on. Our ability to believe in something greater. Not only does it mean every interaction is important; but we are reminded of the pertinence of nurturing all relationships.

...

'You have heard that it was said, "You shall love your neighbor and hate your enemy." But I say to you. Love your enemies and pray for those who persecute you, so that you may be sons of your Father who is in heaven.'

(Matthew 5: 43-48)

...

We hold onto memories. We hold onto pain. We hold onto wrongs committed against us. I have learned life was meant for the opposite. Those who do us wrong. The most beautiful gift we have received is our ability to transform every relationship, every interaction, and every situation. Enemies become kin, family, and friends. One day being able to walk hand in hand. Being able to refer to one another as 'my brother' or 'my sister'.

…

We all are deserving of love. I have made countless mistakes. Lied, cheated, and stolen. I am human. I am imperfect. I continue to seek forgiveness. I continue to seek love. I continue to love every stranger, show appreciation, and mend wounds of travelers. We may not be able to erase past mistakes; but we can improve, change our habits, and remind ourselves as well as others 'we are deserving of love'.

…

‘Before we part ways. I will end today’s letter with this. Despite every misstep. God blessed me. He sent one of his most beautiful, most precious, and most lovely creations. She supports me. She carries me when I am weak, she wipes my tears away. She holds me close. She loves me despite all my scars. She is an angel. I might not deserve what I have; but I will never stop being thankful for what I have…

God sent me an angel that kisses me every day and reminds me.

‘You are loved.’

…

Poem 3: My People, My Kin

Colour. Complexion. Gender.

Identity. Sex. Orientation.

Religion. Ethnicity. Tribe.

Disability. Eye Colour.

Language Spoken.

Country of Origin.

Crimes Committed.

All Are My People.

———

Welcome:

Sinners. Addicts. The 'Ugly'.

Scars. The Abused. The Abuser.

I will fight my way thru hell to find you.

I will drag your ass out of hell past the heavenly gates.

We will share a drink as well as stories.

—

You don't have to be perfect.

You don't have to be 'religious.

You don't have to be a 'law abiding citizen'.

Escorts. Dancers. Thieves.

Kin on death row.

Stop seeking forgiveness from sheep.

Stop seeking acceptance from clowns.

—

If you speak to God.

If you pray to God.

If you cry in front of God.

If you seek forgiveness from God alone.

You are my people.

You are my kin.

—

Law enforcement.

Service members overseas.

Bartenders and waitresses.

Orphans. Widows. Single Fathers.

Children in foster care.

—

Kin sleeping on top of street vents every winter.

Kin digging in trash cans.

Kin begging for change.

You haven't been forgotten.

You are not alone.

You are my people.

You are my kin.

——

Schizophrenia.

Borderline.

Bipolar and Depression.

Alcohol.

Coke.

Heroine and Pornography.

Repeatedly finding yourself in toxic relationship after toxic relationship.

You are my kin.

You are my people.

—

We all make mistakes.

We all are closer to heaven instead of hell.

My people are the folks constantly stepping another step even if the prior step sent them backwards.

Poem 4: Etiquettes of Love

Over the years I have heard.

"I want to be remembered."

"I want to do something great."

"I want to achieve greatness."

What is the foundation of 'greatness' and 'remembrance' made up of…

—

You might have scored 100 points. You might have received 10 gold medals. You might have won 5 championship trophies in a row.

What use is being remembered if you didn't achieve even the simplest dream which is to love others?

We are quick to inflict pain upon our enemies.

We are quick to judge.

Can we not hold others accountable by utilizing etiquettes of love?

—

We do not need to agree to love one another.

We do not need to be of the same complexion to love one another.

We do not need to vote for the same government officials to love one another.

We do not need to strong arm each other regarding gender identity to love one another.

We do not need to be both patriotic to love one another.

We do not need to be attracted to the same gender(s) to love one another.

—

Dreams. Achievements. Fame. Fortune.

They are all materials that crumble in our graves.

Love is forever eternal.

—

Let us paint a picture before we part ways.

I am gender queer. I am two-spirited.

I struggle yet succeed despite living with schizophrenia.

I am one step away from addiction every day.

I am not liberal. I am not conservative. I am pro-life. I believe every individual should receive the right to marry so they are able to experience the pain of divorce.

I believe in the right to bear arms. I believe everyone has the right to defend themselves by any means necessary.

Should you ever hit a woman?

If a woman hits a man, she should be prepared to be treated in the same manner as anyone else.

Self-defense is an equal opportunist.

I never vote based on party.

I always vote based on whether the topic opens doors for those who have been forgotten.

—

On the other end of the table sits a woman.

Jewish by tribe.

Ethiopian by ethnicity.

Humble and courageous.

She believes marriage is between a man and a woman.

She believes in heaven and hell.

She follows her own set of feminist thoughts, theories, and standards.

She waves both the Ethiopian and Israeli flag.

She believes children should be home-schooled.

—

Despite our differences.

Love does not discriminate.

Love breaks down barriers.

Love believes in humility.

Love believes in compassion.

Love allows us both to stand.

Love allows to remind one another.

"I love you."

Short Story 5: Seeing Isn't Believing, Living Is (My Suicide Odyssey)

Most people describe what they see on social media, what they have heard from a friend, and what happens to another person.

Fact is…

I write about what I have lived. I write about each scar I have received since being able to walk on my own two feet.

Most people are confused. You shouldn't fear the one who talks 'big'. You shouldn't fear the one whose goal is to intimidate.

Instead…

You should fear the one who has nothing to lose. You should fear the one who is quiet. You should fear the one who has survived assault after assault. You should fear the one who is continuously seeking peace.

Life. Liberty. The Pursuit of Happiness.

It isn't about giving up; that would be a disgrace to what could have been. It would be a disgrace to who you could have become. It would be a disgrace to what you would have known if you attempted the road less traveled.

I would know…

My life years ago was a clausterfuck. Schizo mom. Abusive father. Adopted at the age ten. Wore a mask in high school. Two suicide attempts. College was a blur.

All I know.

If I would have allowed myself to succumb to regret. If I would have allowed myself to cut my dreams short. I would have never known.

What it felt like to run barefoot upon every continent. What it feels like to participate in sweat lodges. What it feels like to be excited about a simple 'dinner date' with the person you love the most in this world.

If I would have allowed myself to give up…

I would have never known demons should be confronted. I would have never known it is possible to put the pieces back together. I would have never known true love exists. I would have never known love at first sight is not a joke.

Life. Liberty. The Pursuit of Happiness. Heartbreak. Healing. Scars.

Sometimes it feels like the end of the world during moments of chaos and darkness. Truth is if you allow yourself to believe in a brighter future.

Anything is possible.

Poem 6: Chatting with Demons

—

Busy running away from our demons.

Trying so hard to hide.

Sometimes ignoring them.

Seldom do we try to get to know them.

Often,

The fable of the two wolves is misconstrued.

We are told that we need ‘to feed the right wolf’.

—

Do I have to spell it out for you?

We neglect our demons.

Alcoholics aren’t addicts because of alcohol.

Nor do individuals become addicts because of drugs.

Our mental health system, addiction programs, and understanding of sobriety is backwards.

Our answer to addiction is often 'here are safer drugs'.

Our answer to mental health is often 'why don't you try these coping skills'.

We should be focusing on asking and answering the tough questions.

'What fucked you up'.

'How did it fuck you up'.

'How did you react to the fucked-up situation.'

'Do you understand why it is fucked-up.'

'How do you think it can be un-fucked'.

—

Instead of focusing on the trauma.

Instead of focusing on the core struggle.

We are wasting precious time.

Stop focusing on drinks and pre-rolls.

Stop focusing on self-harm and suicide attempts.

They are serious but will repeat if we don't force ourselves to ask ourselves.

—

'Do you have a fucking time machine.'

I don't think so.

We can't change our past, but we can learn from it.

You were young.

You didn't have the skills, strength, or awareness.

Your brain was 1/10th developed.

—

'What can you do differently now'.

'What will help you process the trauma, the tension, and utilize the wrecking ball.'

Mixed martial arts.

Swimming.

Running.

Old fashion baseball bat to abandoned cars.

—

Our demons.

They can lead us into darkness.

They also can be of benefit.

What qualities of yours are toxic?

What habits of yours in the past as well as in the present have caused harm to yourself or others?

—

What have you learned from sitting down and talking with your demons?

For example.

My biological father was an abusive alcoholic when nobody was around.

Both my parents died when I was young.

I have witnessed more bloodshed compared to peace.

Tried to kill myself on three different occasions.

—

If I had ignored my demons.

Only focused on the drugs that I consciously, knowingly, and purposely put in my body.

I would be dead.

Our demons can be helpful.

They are the reason why some of us fight while others flee.

If you are quick to fight.

Easily angered.

Learn to control it.

Utilize it wisely.

If you are quick to sadness.

Understand emotions are not a sign of weakness.

Rather.

They allow us to communicate what we feel.

Demons are often described as.

Tricksters.

Maybe they are.

But not all the time.

Sometimes they are the only ones that have the guts to tell us the truth.

Poem 7: Sundays

If possible.

They should (always) be used as a reflective tool.

Ask important questions.

Ponder the choices you made.

———

What happened this week?

What choices did I make?

Did they benefit me or others?

What were the alternative choices that were available that I did not think of in that moment?

Did I improve as a partner, parent, or friend?

Did I become a better MAN?

Did I learn?

What mistakes did I make?

Did I help others?

Was I selfish?

Was I mindful?

Was I present?

Did I support those who I claim to love?

Did I raise my voice?

Did I resort to physical strength?

Was I patient?

Was I impulsive?

Take time to reflect.

We will continuously make mistakes.

We are imperfect.

The goal isn't perfection.

Instead.

The goal is to learn from our choices at the end of every day.

Accept the fact that improvement is a necessity.

The goal is to do better tomorrow.

Yell less.

Refrain from arguing with clowns.

Every circus needs a clown.

Refrain from exerting physical pain onto others unless the situation requires it.

Be humble.

We are not kings and queens.

We are not ‘royalty’.

We are born into this world needing a caretaker.

Beautifully broken.

Complete and unusual messes.

This is what makes life beautiful.

We have the choice to learn from each other's experiences, choices, and successes.

We can feel pain and be comforted by a stranger.

We can be put back together by a mysterious force called love.

Life is precious.

Life is beautiful.

Life sometimes hurts.

Sometimes it is painful.

Sometimes it feels like it is 'too much to handle'.

Therefore, every Sunday.

If possible.

Heal.

Try again.

Repeat.

Letter 8: Letter to My Children

Let this letter serve as a reminder.

Follow these two rules in life my dear children.

1) Do Not Fear Failure

2) Do Not Allow Others to Confuse Kindness for Weakness

…

If you fear failure; how will you learn from your mistakes?

How can you improve or better yourself if you never fail?

If you lose a match, your team comes in second, or you must tap out.

Refuse to accept a 'participation trophy'.

Instead.

Leave empty handed.

Return home. Train ten times harder. Prepare.

Compete again.

Fear of failure is a coward's attribute.

Don't fear falling.

Don't fear a broken heart.

Don't fear a failing grade.

Failure ignites drive, passion, and motivation.

My dear children.

Do not fear pain.

Do not fear scraping your knee.

Do not fear be alone nor silence.

Be patient.

Understand.

You can be 'alone' yet not feel 'lonely'.

Fear of failure is not worth the depression, sadness, nor anxiety.

My dear children.

We are born as ‘imperfect creation’ and will die as ‘imperfect creation’.

Accept, appreciate, and love your scars.

Allow your pain to produce humility.

Feed both your positive and negative qualities.

Both wolves need to be fed.

…

My dear children.

Do not allow others to confuse kindness for weakness.

Be kind.

Be sincere.

Be gentle.

Be humble.

Know your strength.

Practice patience.

Strength and power are not tests of who is the most impatient or most impulsive.

Instead.

True strength and true power are the ability to inflict the minimalist amount of pain necessary of which the situation dictates.

Be kind to yourself.

Allow those who around you to ‘talk big’.

Allow those around you to feel ‘powerful’.

Wisdom easily defeats strength.

Draw lines in the sand.

If someone overextends.

If they lay hands on you, your children, your parents, your dog(s), or step onto your property after being told they are not welcome.

My dear children.

Allow those who confuse kindness for weakness to experience as well as to learn the truth.

Only inflict the required amount of pain that the situation dictates.

Clearly demonstrate the message.

“I am not one to be fucked with.”

My dear children.

Learn how to hold a rifle.

Learn how to grapple.

Learn how to take a couple licks.

Learn how to hunt.

Learn how to skin an animal.

Learn how to defend yourself.

Learn how to defend your home.

Learn how to inflict the required amount pain that the situation dictates without having to call the police.

Learn how to be patient.

Learn how to be calculated.

Learn ‘strength’ is not ‘power’.

Pretend to be weak when you are strong.

Pretend to be unsteady when you are prepared

My dear children.

Your father made mistakes.

If you learn anything from me.

Family. Kin. Defend Your Property.

The Right to Bear Arms.

Love Your Mother.

Letter 9: How Schizophrenia Impacts My Day to Day

I am writing this as a pre-caution.

Put simply.

It is my medicine walk.

My only request.

Don't interpret it as a warning.

My thoughts are pure, sincere, and free.

Once every few months; I have a weeklong stretch in which my schizophrenia transforms into Atlas from Greek mythology.

Condemned to hold up the sky for eternity.

Waking up anxious.

Attempting to eat while voices, shadows, and characters speak ill of me, of the dead, and of those I love.

Working, driving, and socializing.

Trying to show appreciation to all those love me, speak sincerely, and understand the importance of humility.

———

Twenty-four hours a day I am bombarded with words, phrases, and commands.

I hear, see, smell, taste, and feel what others ignore.

This is not a plea or a cry for help.

Instead.

It is a love letter to all those willing to listen.

———

I am aware.

I am present.

I can compare what others see with what my eyes, ears, and mind witness.

I remember as a child having ‘invisible friends.

I remember in high school playing chess with ‘make believe friends.

I remember in college spending weeks in psychiatric wards.

I am not dangerous.

I am not violent.

I am human.

I ask all who read this to read sincerely.

Schizophrenia has turned my life upside down.

Imagine trying to concentrate while a circus performs in your living room, bedroom, at your office, in a cafe, or while you are on the phone.

Sometimes I pray.

Sometimes I wish my eyes closed and never opened.

Letter 10: Why Do I Love Liz

———

I am not describing the usual romantic bullshit or butterflies.

What does Liz do that is irreplaceable?

What qualities does Liz have that make her special?

What are the things Liz does that no one else can do, won't do, or have never done?

———

For starters…

My mania doesn't scare her.

She never ran away.

When I am manic, she is calm, patient, and loving.

She continues to love me despite all my weaknesses.

She continues to love me despite the voices I hear.

She didn’t run away after I told her that I was diagnosed with schizophrenia during my freshman year of college.

It didn’t scare her.

Instead…

She asked questions.

Liz didn’t run away after learning of my past addiction, trouble staying sober, and traumatic childhood.

——

So…

Why do I love Liz?

She is what I would describe as a ‘ride or die old lady’.

Not many of them left.

They are descendants of the Old World.

Liz comes from a line of warriors, spiritual leaders, and healers.

They refused to quit despite hardships endured.

Liz is one of the few that remain.

———

We live in a time that is defined by a 50 percent divorce rate.

We live in a time that is defined by lawyers, court, and materials.

So…

Why do I love Liz?

She is everything I am not.

She is everything I don't deserve.

She is everything I prayed for.

———

Poem 11: Unexpected Beauty

I have lived life which is probably why I walk the line.

When you have shaken hands.

Walked hand in hand with death.

Living life as well as loving life makes a whole lot more sense.

These feet have walked thousands of miles.

Our vision was meant to witness beauty.

Hands meant to heal.

If only life was that simple.

Truth be told.

I have climbed mountains.

Sat on the edge overlooking the abyss.

Usually, the abyss is described as darkness combined with a little bit of depression.

Not me though.

I find beauty in the most unexpected places.

Witnessed miracles performed by strangers wearing ripped and dirty rags.

Watched smiles perform heart surgery.

I have walked upon volcanic soil.

Walked thru jungle terrain.

Across deserts.

Discussed the purpose of life with orcas.

Held baby cheetahs in my arms.

Wrestled with bear cubs.

Meditated in the most beautiful Buddhist temples.

Prayed in the most breathtaking mosques, synagogues, and churches.

I have witnessed families feeding strangers, providing a warm bed, and cash the next day.

———

Beauty is something special.

It cannot be defined nor articulated.

It must be experienced.

It must be felt.

It must be witnessed.

———

Walking the line isn't about putting yourself in danger.

Walking the line is about opening your heart, mind, body, and soul to others, Mother Nature, and The Great Spirit.

It is about respecting the soil under our feet.

It is about loving your neighbor, orphans, widows, and the poor.

Walking the line is about finding beauty in unexpected places.

An unknown comic performing at a comedy club.

Slow dancing with a friend or your lover while it rains.

Walking the line is about standing up to bullies, spreading love to the forgotten, and spreading positivity.

———

You don't need to be single in order to show appreciation.

Fuck the norms.

It is a beautiful thing when you can speak candidly.

'Honey. What do you think? They got some cake.'

Walking the line.

It is a beautiful act.

It is spiritual.

It is an act of worship.

God Bless.

———

Poem 12: I Wish Love Was the Reason

—

Despite having the reasons,

I never seized believing.

You wouldn’t believe me.

The number of times I have held the hands of children, mothers, and fathers.

Trying to understand why bad things happen to good people.

—

You can see it.

It is a memory that never fades.

It never gets old.

It can never be forgotten.

Everything will be alright.

Amid chaos.

Light exists.

I have witnessed Israelis and Palestinians embrace.

Cry together.

I have witnessed Sunnis and Shias eat from the same plate.

Sing together.

I have witnessed the most ‘racist’ befriend and marry the opposite complexion.

Laugh together.

Unfortunately.

A lot of folks in our world don’t want such goodness to exist.

They enjoy chaos.

Fortunately.

Love is the strongest weapon.

It cannot be destroyed nor ‘invented’.

Love.

It was handcrafted.

Signed.

Sealed.

And delivered.

———

Poem 13: You Are Gorgeous

———

Different shapes, sizes, and complexions.

Scars, memories, traumas, and experiences.

Misfits, midgets, fags, and witches.

Flat ass, no ass, and a small chest.

Freckles, acne, and hairy legs.

We all are beautiful.

We all are gorgeous.

Beautiful people.

Rainbow complexion.

Cracker motherfuckers to black motherfuckers.

———

Short hair.

Long hair.

Dresses like a God-fearing Mormon.

Loves twerking.

Receiving tips.

Buck-toothed with a double chin.

You might be overweight or underweight.

You might be in rehab or need to go to rehab.

You might be deaf, blind, or daft.

You are beautiful.

You are gorgeous.

Lazy eye.

Maybe you are fucking crazy.

Maybe you just enjoy fucking crazy.

Maybe you were incarcerated.

Maybe you still are incarcerated.

We all have made bad choices.

We all will make bad choices.

Maybe you lied, cheated, and stole.

Nobody is perfect.

We all are beautiful.

We should put in the effort to improve mentally, physically, and spiritually.

Despite these facts.

You are gorgeous.

Small feet.

Small dick.

Small hands

Uncoordinated.

Opposite of athletic.

Maybe you love dresses.

Maybe you love pink.

Maybe you love wearing pink dresses.

Maybe you love painting your nails instead of participating in ‘gym class’.

My only suggestion.

Learn how to change a flat tire, check your engine oil, defend yourself, shoot a gun, shake your ass, and drive a stick shift.

You are gorgeous.

You could have a stutter.

You could be unhygienic.

You could be homeless.

You could have schizophrenia.

You could be a widow.

You could be an orphan.

You could be a survivor of domestic abuse.

You could be an exotic dancer.

You could be a ‘professional’.

You could be a ‘sugar baby’.

You could be trans, non-binary, or identify as a fucking unicorn.

None-the-less.

You are gorgeous.

Poem 14: It Is OK, Be Yourself

Heartbreak followed by a bottle of pills.

Heartbreak followed by a dozen shots of whiskey.

Receiving hundreds of messages, a week.

'You are going to hell if you don't repent.'

It is okay.

Remember.

It is okay.

Sometimes it is going to hurt like hell.

Despite all the pain.

It is okay.

Despite every scar.

It is okay.

It is up to you.

Take it or leave it.

I am only but a man.

I have cried.

I have fallen.

I have witnessed children laugh who witnessed genocide.

I have held the hand of widows, orphans, and thieves.

It is okay.

This life is temporary.

Daylight subsides.

Nightfall arrives.

It is okay.

Be yourself.

Love your physique.

Love your curves.

Love your scars.

Love every memory.

Dark days and bright days.

Love the good.

Love the bad.

Love the ugly.

Believe in yourself.

Deliver yourself from evil.

———

It is okay.

Focus on you.

Self-care.

Be selfish.

Not everyone is going to like you.

Not everyone is going to agree with you.

Not everyone is going to accept you.

It is okay.

———

Only Fans.

Nudes.

Exotic dancer.

Travel frequently.

Leave the cult.

Stop believing.

It is okay.

Be yourself.

Fuck the sheep.

Do not follow.

Be yourself.

It is okay.

Poem 15: Southern Blessings

…..

Nothing is wrong with living simply.

I love fried chicken, biscuits and gravy, peach cobbler, drinking shine, and conversing with others about the beauty of Jesus, nature, and God while drinking beer.

Barbeques, cookouts, and church.

Treating people decent, respecting others despite our differences, and acknowledging difference of opinions are what make us unique.

…..

For example.

I find men to be physically as well as sexually more attractive compared to women.

Yet.

I love my Old Lady.

It only took me 60 seconds to realize.

She is the only One that I want to get old with, sleep next to, laugh, cry, and converse about the old days with.

I am not liberal nor am I conservative.

I learned a long time ago.

Majority of events, experiences, and feelings are situational, individual, and morally gray.

One of the most beautiful Southern blessings I received at a young age, attempt to practice daily, and will forever hold dear to my heart.

"Love is patient, love is kind. It does not envy, it does not boast, it is not proud. It does not dishonor others, it is not self-seeking, it is not easily angered, it keeps no record of wrongs."

(1 Corinthians 13: 4-5)

.....

I love my neighbors. I love my enemies. I love my kin.

Growing up.

We were raised proper.

Respect your mother, father, neighbors, and remember.

If you are caught fooling around.

They don't have to be your momma', daddy, or siblings to whoop you.

It could be one of your teachers, a classmate's auntie, or the bodega clerk down the street.

"Above all, keep loving one another earnestly, since love covers a multitude of sins."

(1 Peter 4:8)

Don't take this the wrong way.

This is important.

Love, self-defense, and boundaries are not mutually exclusive.

I might love you.

But.

That does not mean I am going allow you to walk over me.

It is because I love you that boundaries will be set.

It is because I love you that if you cross or impede upon the boundaries constructed, I will defend with no hesitation myself, my safety, my security, my kin's safety, my kin's security, my dog, my home, and my possessions.

…..

You might disagree me.

Hell.

Majority of individual probably will disagree.

But.

I consider all my statements as Southern Blessings.

Whether it was due to a miracle, good tidings, or persevering through struggle, chaos, and darkness.

Most importantly.

It is about spreading love, positivity, and good ‘vibes.

“And above all these put-on love, which binds everything together in perfect harmony.”

(Colossians 3:14)

Compliment others.

Send good tidings.

Receive every blessing with a smile.

You could be married. You could be single. You could be divorced.

You could be in your 60’s. You could be a freshman in college.

Be yourself. Be true to you.

If someone. If anybody. If the whole damn world.

Doesn’t like how you speak, look, dress, think, or feel.

Honestly.

Fuck em'.

Distance yourself.

Leave all of them' high and dry.

Don't look back.

Keep driving.

It is all outta' love.

We are going to end today's conversation.

Spend the cause of Allah and do not contribute to your destruction with your own hands, but do good, for Allah loves those who do good (virtuous).

(Surah Al-Baqarah 2:195)

.....

Poem 16: Definition of Love (My Old Lady)

White Trash Conservative.

Jamaican Light Skinned Clinician.

Free at last.

BBQ, Moonshine, Buddha, Jesus, and Country Music.

Show respect.

Receive respect.

First time we greeted one another.

Her aura, light, and love caused the Northern Light's to experience jealousy for the first time.

She was the one.

She is the one.

Always will be.

____

We handle things differently.

She’s gentle.

I was raised to fight first.

Seek answers to my questions later.

She’s easy to love.

I was raised to protect myself.

Defended my sanity up until we looked into each other’s eyes.

Two different people.

One love.

Two different methods.

Share love.

Two different upbringings.

Spread love.

It is our hearts, minds, and medicine hands that constantly remind, heal, and comfort one another.

I swear like a sailor.

Love moonshine. Greasy food. Fried chicken. Lemonade. Biscuits and Gravy.

Jeans.

Boots.

Flannel.

Stories for days.

Scars on most of my limbs.

Sometimes I am judgmental.

I suffer from imperfection.

Somehow.

For some reason.

You see past my weaknesses.

Every fucked-up experience.

Twisted dark days.

You gave me a chance.

Blessed me with a gentle shoulder to lean on.

It worked.

You are my one and only weakness.

Some people will be confused.

What does 'white trash' have to do with being 'two-spirited' and 'finding love'?

Respect + Love + Appreciation + Struggle + Blessings + Wisdom + Wakan Tanka…

Equals.

Happiness.

Some settle for less.

I refuse.

God granted me the ability to put in more so that I can receive more.

One hell of a woman.

Ball of fire.

Able to go from ‘0’ to ‘100’ in 3 seconds.

When someone asks for assistance

She’s the first to jump in and start the car.

She will call you out every time you start talking bullshit.

Mentally. Physically. Spirituality.

She transcends beauty.

_____

I might never be rich, wealthy, or famous.

Only thing I care about.

Only person I care about.

Doing everything I can do so that when we lay down.

We can speak three simple words.

I.

Love.

You.

____

Journal Entry 17: November 20th, 2022

We don't need to pretend to be fortune tellers.

We don't have to pretend to know the future.

We don't need to open old wounds.

———

To know. To be sure. To be confident. To believe. To have faith.

You need.

It requires.

Two pieces.

First.

Practicing being physically present in the now.

Second.

Befriending patience.

These two steps. These two attributes. These two skills.

They suggest one will endure hardship.

Physical. Mental. And Spiritual.

Most people give up.

As soon as something requires strength, perseverance, pain, and courage.

Most walk away.

Most hide in bed.

Don’t be like the rest.

Be different.

Choose wisely.

Trust the process.

Failure. Defeat. Struggle.

Learn from each crosswalk.

Triumph. Happiness. Rewards. Blessings. Treasures.

Blessings follow effort.

Lessons follow courage.

Knowledge requires implementation.

———

True passion.

Whether love, work, or pleasure.

All three.

Require passion.

If you don't have or feel passion for 'X'.

Majority of rationale folks give up.

———

Learn to smile.

Learn to laugh.

Learn to welcome struggle.

Prerequisite for lived experience.

Smile during painful moments.

Laugh while depressed.

Remember.

Shining stars encompass the night sky.

Poem 18: 'Ashwiyaa'

For a long time, I was drowning.

For a long time, I was running.

Everything changed.

You caught me in my feelings while I was interacting with demons.

After our first night together.

I knew you were the one.

'Ashwiyaa'

In the beginning I constantly was fighting demons.

My desire to run away.

My desire to disappear.

It all changed the moment you wrapped me up in your arms.

My heart felt a warm embrace for the first time in a long time.

It had been ages.

I had forgotten what it felt like.

Imagine, a child witnessing a sunrise.

Losing his sight shortly after.

Regaining his sight at the age of 31.

First thing he witnesses is a sunrise.

It would be the most beautiful sunrise he ever witnessed.

____

That is how I feel when I am with you.

I feel loved.

I feel valuable.

I feel precious.

You are everything.

You are my everything.

You mean everything to me.

Every one of your scars.

Every one of your imperfections.

Every one of your tears.

Every time you laugh.

Every time you smile.

Every time we make love.

Every time you ride.

Every time we kiss.

You are my everything.

You are everything to me.

You mean everything to me.

Poem 19: Miss You All

It has been a while. We haven’t talked for quite some time.

A lot of people don’t understand. You can tell by the way they describe suicide.

“Fate.”

“It was his or her time.”

Bullshit.

Unless you are elderly. Lived a full life. Travelled the world. It is never “your time”.

All the memories.

Love 24/7.

Abdullah. Ten years old. Street kid. Sold DVDs to tourist. He always made me laugh.

Corny fucking jokes. Dad jokes for sure.

Becca. Most people afraid of her. Properly trained. License to kill. No fucking joke. Heart of gold. She would do everything and anything. She hated board games and puzzles. Every time I asked if she wanted to join. She replied, “absolutely bitch. I was waiting for you to ask”.

Teresa. She loved tequila. No joke. Could hold her own. One hell of a dancer. Hips were hypnotizing. No joke. At the end of every night. She refused every offer. Blessed me with the honor of walking her home.

I miss you all.

www.ingramcontent.com/pod-product-compliance
Lightning Source LLC
LaVergne TN
LVHW082250150826
845677LV00009B/1589
9798375124148